ARTIFICIAL INTELLIGENCE

THE

NEW GOLD

AI is a money-printing machine.

BY

JEFFREY DAHMER

COPYRIGHT

Copyright © 2023 by JEFFREY DAHMER

Table of Contents

INTRODUCTION

AI is a money-printing machine.

A modern-day gold rush is underway, and it has nothing to do with precious metals; it has everything to do with artificial intelligence (AI). AI has emerged as the new gold in today's quickly expanding technology world, and businesses are racing to establish their claims.

The Artificial Intelligence Gold Rush

The present AI rush, like the gold rushes of yesteryear, is motivated by the huge potential value of this transformational technology. Companies across industries are emphasizing AI, seeing it as the key to future success and competitive advantage.

As a result, organizations throughout the globe are increasing their investments in AI and competing for top personnel in the sector.

Healthcare businesses, for example, are significantly investing in AI, with the technology promising to improve patient care and illness detection. AI-powered solutions are being developed. utilized to evaluate enormous volumes of health data, helping to anticipate disease outbreaks, monitor patient health in real time, and create individualized treatment plans.

Similarly, the industrial industry is using AI to optimize output, enhance quality control, and forecast equipment breakdowns. AI is used by companies such as General Electric to examine machine data, allowing them to identify possible equipment faults and arrange preventive maintenance.

This cross-sector adoption of AI highlights its critical role in contemporary business, similar to a gold rush, where the 'gold' is the plethora of options that AI provides.

However, most people are unaware of how to capitalize on this opportunity.

I'll show you the three greatest methods to generate money using artificial intelligence in 2023.

Become an AI Expert and Profit from
Your Experience

Become an AI Expert and Profit from Your Experience

AI professionals are paid $350,000 per year by companies.

Better better, leverage your AI expertise to advise with and educate others how to use AI.

1. AI and Machine Learning Foundations

"Create a comprehensive guide for individuals just starting out in artificial intelligence." Dive into the fundamental principles, techniques, and history of artificial intelligence. Distinguish between AI, machine learning, and deep learning. Hands-on activities are advised towards the conclusion. readings, and techniques for lifelong learning in an ever-changing area."

Advantage: Provides a good foundation for anybody wishing to begin their AI knowledge path.

2. Advanced AI Algorithms and Techniques

"Create a meticulous guide for those who want to delve deeper into advanced AI techniques." Talk about neural networks, reinforcement learning, and natural language processing. Provide information about the most recent research, prospective uses, and problems. Finish with hands-on projects, case studies, and tools for remaining up to speed on AI advances."

Advantage: Advances pupils' AI competence from intermediate to advanced levels.

3. Real-World AI Projects and Portfolio Development

"Delve deeply into a detailed plan for individuals who want to demonstrate their AI expertise through practical projects." Suggest a variety of tasks ranging from beginner to advanced. to advanced levels, covering a wide range of topics such as finance, healthcare, and entertainment. Highlight project documentation tools, outcomes showing tactics, and strategies for developing an outstanding AI portfolio."

Advantage: Assists students in showing their abilities and obtaining future customers or companies.

4. Consulting to monetize AI expertise

"Create a comprehensive blueprint for AI experts interested in venturing into consulting." Discuss the environment of AI consulting, possible client industries, and fee-setting tactics. Emphasize the value of networking, developing a personal brand, and maintaining client relationships. Finish with tools for successful consultancy management, contract templates, and market research resources."

Benefit: Assists AI specialists in converting their expertise into a viable consulting business.

5. Developing and Marketing AI Courses

"Create a niche for yourself." A precise method for AI specialists who want to share their expertise via online courses. Examine course production tools, curriculum design, and tactics for delivering compelling information. Talk about possible obstacles, promoting your course, and getting student feedback. Finish with examples of successful AI courses, revenue techniques, and tools for ongoing course enhancement."

Find and Implement an AI Side Hustle

AI has made it simpler than ever to establish your own side hustle and expand quickly.

Identify an issue, then utilize AI technologies to create an AI SaaS that addresses it.

Another possibility is to develop specialist AI. stuff on X, YouTube, or even your own audience.

1. Looking for AI Side Hustle Opportunities

"Create a comprehensive guide for enthusiasts interested in exploring side hustle opportunities in the AI domain." Investigate market trends, industry needs, and prospective niches in depth. Highlight topics such as data analytics, chatbot development, and artificial intelligence content production. Finish with brainstorming activities and market research tools. as well as ways for establishing distinct value propositions."

Benefit: Assists people in discovering profitable AI side hustle possibilities that are market-driven.

2. AI Side Hustle Planning and Prioritization

"Create a meticulous blueprint for people who want to balance their full-time job with an AI side hustle." Discuss time management skills, goal planning, and the value of constant learning. Provide advice on how to prevent burnout, manage various obligations, and create limits. Finish with productivity tools, time-tracking strategies, and project management resources."

Benefit: Provides ideas for successfully balancing a side hustle with other responsibilities.

3. Create an MVP for Your AI Idea

"Delve deeply into a detailed plan for individuals eager to turn their AI side hustle idea into a tangible product," says the prompt.

Discuss the concepts of Minimum Viable Product (MVP) creation, iterative testing, and gathering user input. Provide quick prototype methodologies, possible hazards to avoid, and MVP development tools. Finish with case studies, MVP launch tactics, and tools for getting early user input."

Advantage: Assists enthusiasts in transforming their AI concept into a concrete and tested product.

4. Marketing and Promotion of Your Artificial Intelligence Solution

"Develop a solid strategy for individuals looking to market their AI side hustle solution to a larger audience." Dive into digital marketing methods, content production, and social media exploitation. Emphasize the significance of developing an online presence, networking, and partnerships. Finish with tools for measuring marketing performance, audience engagement techniques, and resources for further marketing education."

Benefit: Individuals may use this tool to efficiently advertise their AI service and reach out to prospective consumers.

5. Pricing and Revenue Generation for Your AI Service or Product

"Create a detailed blueprint for side hustlers looking to monetize their AI service or product." Talk about price tactics, value propositions, and market research methods. Provide information on freemium models, subscription programs, and prospective income sources. Finish with payment processing tools, discount or promotion methods, and resources for analyzing market price dynamics."

Benefit: Offers advice on how to properly price and monetize AI services or goods.

Create AI Chatbots and Automations for Increased Efficiency and Savings

Create AI Chatbots and Automations for Increased Efficiency and Savings

You may keep it simple by utilizing no-code alternatives.,

alternatively you may invest the effort to study VoiceFlow, Botpress, Stack AI, and other AI chatbot building platforms.

Focus on Zapier connections and how you can help improve a company's particular workflow for AI automations.

1. AI Chatbot Development Fundamentals

"Create a comprehensive introduction to AI chatbot development for businesses looking to improve customer interactions." Investigate fundamental principles in design. concepts, and the advantages of AI-driven chat conversations. Finally, hands-on activities, tool suggestions, and methods for integrating chatbots into current corporate platforms will be presented."

Benefit: Gives enterprises a basic grasp of the potential and execution of AI chatbots.

2. Creating Chatbot Conversations That Are Easy to Use

"Create a meticulous guide focused on creating intuitive and user-friendly AI chatbot conversations." Investigate the psychology of user interactions, conversational flows, and ways for dealing with complicated questions. Finally, provide best practices, tools for testing chatbot UX, and resources for ongoing chatbot design improvement."

Benefit: Ensures that the chatbot offers a fluid and intuitive conversational experience to users.

3. Chatbot Integration with Business Systems

"Delve deeply into a detailed plan for businesses wishing to integrate AI chatbots with existing systems such as CRMs." Databases and e-commerce platforms are two examples. Emphasize API integrations, data synchronization, and possible issues. Provide seamless integration solutions, monitoring tools, and information for addressing typical integration challenges."

Benefit: Allows for the seamless integration of chatbots, improving company processes and data flow.

4. Artificial Intelligence-Driven Business Process Automation

"Draft a comprehensive guide for businesses considering AI-driven automation for repetitive tasks and processes." Examine areas ideal for automation, accessible technologies, and possible cost reductions. Discuss obstacles, successful automation rollout tactics, and approaches for monitoring and enhancing automated operations. Finally, include case studies, ROI calculation methodologies, and tools for remaining current on automation developments."

Benefit: Allows organizations to improve processes, decrease manual labor, and save significantly on costs.

5. Analytics and Continuous Improvement for Chatbots

"Create a" is the prompt. A complete framework for organizations to successfully monitor and assess chatbot performance. Examine measures such as customer satisfaction, resolution rate, and interaction time. Provide insights on chatbot analytics tools, user feedback methodologies, and approaches for continuous chatbot enhancement. Finish with tangible strategies for iterative improvements, A/B testing approaches, and sophisticated chatbot analytics resources."

Advantage: Allows organizations to constantly enhance chatbot functionality, assuring optimum user pleasure.

www.ingramcontent.com/pod-product-compliance
Lightning Source LLC
Chambersburg PA
CBHW061100050326
40690CB00012B/2681